A Walk in the Desert

J.P. Amy

To order additional copies of this book, contact:
Xlibris
844-714-8691
www.Xlibris.com
Orders@Xlibris.com

ISBN: Softcover   979-8-3694-3827-5
            Hardcover   979-8-3694-3828-2
            EBook   979-8-3694-3826-8

Print information available on the last page

Rev. date: 01/09/2025

A YELLOW BALL IN

A BLUE SKY.

4

RED SAND PURPLE
MOUNTAINS HIGH

WIND BLOWING TUMBLE
WEEDS ROLLING

A PLACE WHERE CACTUS
AND FLOWERS GROW.

A TARANTULA AND
A SCORPION CREEPY
CRAWLING EVER SO SLOW.

A GOLDEN EAGLE SOARING.

A HOT AIR BALLOON

ROARING.

A RIVER RUNS DRY,
A RAVEN'S CRY

A COYOTE'S HOWL, A JACK
RABBIT RUNNING FROM
A GREAT HORNED OWL

A HORNY TOAD
IN THE ROAD.

A MOUSE TRYING TO
ESCAPE, A RATTLESNAKE.

A MOUNTAIN BLUEBIRD IN A
JUNIPER TREE, A BIG BLACK
AND YELLOW BUMBLE BEE

A ROADRUNNER
RACING A LIZARD.

WHO WILL BE THE WINNER?

THE END

THE SUN IS GOING DOWN!

TIME TO GET HOME
FOR DINNER!

KNME
TV 5

Eighth Annual National Contest

Local Contest Funding Provided by:

1ST FIRST STATE BANK Wendy's

ALBUQUERQUE JOURNAL

READING RAINBOW®

Young Writers & Illustrators Contest

Certificate of Achievement

This certifies that

James Amy

has submitted an original story to the **2002** Young Writers & Illustrators Awards Contest and has officially earned the honorary title, **Reading Rainbow** Young Writer & Illustrator.

LeVar Burton

Printed in the United States
by Baker & Taylor Publisher Services